Dec. 03.

To

3e

GW01090545

a flight of writers

To Joan
Best Wishes

a flight of writers

CLUAIN MEALA WRITERS' ANTHOLOGY

RECTORY PRESS

Published by
Rectory Press
Portlaw, Co. Waterford, Ireland.

ISBN: 1 903698 06 7

Design by Paul Callanan.

Contents

A word from the editor

There are groups of writers coming together across the world, from Minesota to Miltown Malbay, from Connemara to Clonmel. To contemplate the sheer volume of work, of words, produced by these thousands of groups would be overwhleming, daunting beyond measure. You have to ask, what is happening here? Why are so many people being compelled to take up pens and spend hours alone mining themselves for words?

The need to come together as a group is understandable. Writers seek out their own kind and within the group find support, encouragement and editorial reflection. Yet the urge to write is inexplicable. More than a need to make sense of the world around us, writing is an attempt to articulate the vague, nebulous territory of the personal voice: the soul. For many writers this task is as necessary as breathing, more so even, for not to write endangers the health and well-being of the poet, the short story writer, the novelist.

The work in this anthology gives space to the many different voices of the Cluain Meala Writers' Group. It reflects the unpredictable, rebellious nature of the muse that moves through writers. Sometimes it wants to be funny, sometimes dramatic, cool, demanding, angry or tender.

In her poem 'Theft', the poet Mary O'Gorman visits Gozo's citadel, she tells us that on 'cell walls are pictures of galleys, a mast added for each year served', yet in cell three an unidentified prisoner has 'carved a sun'. One can only guess at the limited tools he had available to him to create such an image. The Cluain Meala writers often work under similar pressure, with such limits, squeezing time between the demands of jobs, families and responsibilities. They come to the page with the tools of reality and experience, memory and longing, and onto the invisible boundaries which define and connect all our lives, they are leaving their mark.

Grace Wells
Literature Officer
South Tipperary Arts Centre

Anne-Marie Magorrian
Johnny-No-Name

It wasn't the first time — Johnny's irritation jagged through his body causing him to twitch and jerk. He sat helpless and naked on the commode chair, a small towel draped over his lap. The bathroom was crowded, he had to wait for his shower. His dark broody eyes surveyed the queue of shrivelled semi-naked Oldies. Some yelled, others beat their spindly hands against the walls or commodes or even themselves. Others sat quietly, accepting the routine of their daily lives. They had no choice. They were cared for, kept alive and safe, but they would never walk free. Their former lives were a distant dream. Age and the demons it brought with it had whipped the vitality and health out of them. The inevitable rhythm of pause-stop-stagnate had taken over.

Lynne was Johnny's care-worker. Large, bad-tempered and rough. She loathed him and he knew it only too well. Mostly he would behave but this morning he felt agitated and claustrophobic. Lynne shifted uncomfortably in the humid heat and beads of stinging sweat dripped into her eyes. She swore at the other care-workers for not rushing through the shower routine.

'Get a move on there, I've a no-hoper Abo, here giving me an ear bashing!' She yelled.

Johnny spat at her and missed. She spun around and punched him. Her big white fist smashed into his left cheek. His head bounced off the metal rim of the chair back. Anger, frustration and sorrow almost melted down his mind and he roared. Shaking uncontrollably Johnny swore and stuttered before dropping his head. The hiss of the showers seemed to calm him. He knew the welt on his throbbing face would not show through his black skin. Who would believe him? Who cared? A connection couldn't be made. Too many links missing. 'Tea, tea,' he sobbed, as Lynne roughly wheeled him under the shower-head. The other care-workers discreetly turned away.

Johnny No-Name, was guessed to be thirty years old. An Aboriginal resident at St James Nursing Home, in the popular holiday resort of Cairns, North Queensland. He was a stocky five-foot man with a crazy mane of black wiry hair. His balance was poor and he shuffled along slowly often swaying and falling. He needed to link on to someone but was obstinate and mostly helped himself by holding on to the metal handrail that ran the length of the corridor. He liked this slow walka-bout. He could imagine he was strolling home. To where, he wasn't quite sure as his memory had been cast into a dark space and he could not retrieve it.

Johnny had been found lying alone under a golden wattle tree in Flecker Botanic Gardens north of town. He was bruised and beaten. His body was a mangle of raw flesh and blood oozed from a deep gash across his cheek. 'Sharp instrument', the police had concluded. Several brown bottles lay scattered alongside his motionless body. They smelt of strong spirit, meths perhaps or homebrew. They had not analysed it. 'He's lucky to be alive,' the doctor had grunted, 'long-term nursing care needed'.

Nobody had explained to Johnny what had happened. During those first few months he was hoisted from bed to bath to toilet to chair. They spoon-fed him pureed mixtures - vile and tasteless. He might choke, no time for ongoing assessment. 'Simplify, reduce the risk.' Dictated matron.

9

His sight was hazy, his words floated out disconnected and without much meaning. He was trouble, at the nursing home, 'bad-tempered and volatile'. These words had reached his ears at the report hand-overs at the nurses' station. They thought he couldn't hear or make sense of it all. The induction of new staff members always included a character assassination of Johnny, usually seated only a mere few feet away. He would lower his head as the derogatory terms pricked in a way he could not understand. Without warning he would lift anything he could find, usually his comforting cup of tea, and throw it in the direction of the piercing arrows. This was followed by punishment,. 'No tea for you Johnny for another hour. We are putting you to your room until you agree to behave'. 'No tea, no tea', he wailed as they roughly pushed him into a wheelchair or commode, whatever was at hand with wheels, and sped down to his room. No comfort there. A small room, painted white, bed, wardrobe and chair. Clinical, sticky and bare. The fan whirred overhead. He slept and escaped.

Johnny loved sitting on the veranda. Most afternoons they walked him out there. He would hesitate, breathe deeply and point to an old cane chair with a yellow pillow. His chair. There he would sit and gaze over the lush landscape towards the hills and rainforest. As a child he had bathed there in cool shaded waterholes. He had dived under arcs of majestic waterfalls with their spray of rainbows. Heady intoxicating scents burst from vibrant plants and bushes cascading over the rocks. Noisy pink galas, sulphur-crested cockatoos, lorikeets and the raucous guffaw of the kookaburras echoed throughout the rainforest. They would never judge him, punish him or hurt him. Johnny stayed out until sunset. He loved the brief twilight. The sky was splashed with red, orange, powder blue and mauve. The hills were a misty violet hue until the night sky spilled over a deep velvet black. Switch off time for Johnny.

Early February was unusually stormy. Rumours of a cyclone circulated. Panic set in. Staff were tense, edgy and frightened. New bulletins flashed across the droning TV's advising people to stay calm and stock up on batteries, food and bottled water. Cyclone Eddie shifted around gathering pace one hundred miles out at sea creating havoc along the coastline of North Queensland. The wind moaned and an eerie whine pierced the air. Trees crashed and debris scattered along the deserted streets. Johnny felt very ill that evening, his pulse raced and sweat trickled down his body saturating his thin faded pyjamas. His head pounded and his tongue seemed to swell, filling his mouth so that he could not speak. He was frightened and confused. No-one stopped by to check in on him. Too early, he supposed. He felt more alone now than ever before and a tear escaped. His breathing faded.

Splashes of colour swirled around him, spinning, merging, giddy and wild. Out of the melange, faces formed. Caring faces, painted and patterned. A hand stretched out and gently took his. His mind sharpened as a potent energy surged through his limp body in a rush of warmth. He felt strong and brave like a warrior before battle. The Sky Heroes had come to guide him back to the Dreaming. Johnny glanced back. Lynne had looked in - too late. She bent over his cooling ashen shell that lay on the bed and gently wiped his tear-stained face. 'Farewell Johnny No-Name,' she whispered, 'safe journey and may your God forgive you.'

Mary O'Gorman
Theft

I place my palm over the outline of yours
in soft Maltese limestone. Touch where
you carved *Guiseppe 1809*. Wonder how
long you were entombed in Gozo's Citadel.

Your crime is not recorded but a guide
tells me you were a fisherman
who may have stolen wheat
or fruit for your family.

On other cell walls are pictures of galleys,
a mast added for each year served.
But here in cell 3, you carved a sun.
I hope that, whatever your crime,

its rays sometimes blazed
in the darkness and you basked
near olive trees
and yellow-throated crocus

or fished from your small boat
in Ramla Bay
watched only by blue-rock thrushes
and children collecting shells.

Mary O'Gorman
The Heron and the Hot Tub

I'm the Brad Pitt of herons.
I chill out on the river Suir
My pad is outside Carrick
but some days I am lured

by the thought of a Clonmel bird
who lives near Davis Road.
So I tell the wife a long-billed lie
'bout bringing home tasty toads.

I put on dark sunglasses,
gel my long black plume.
Flap casually on upstream -
such a real cool dude.

Stop by the Leisure Centre.
Snack on frogs and eels.
Am munching on a tasty trout
when I notice rising steam

coming from a wooden construction,
some type of human nest.
People are sitting in it
in a state of near undress.

Their loud talking and laughing
has terrified the fish.
Though ducks don't seem to be disturbed
but ducks were always thick.

12

Nearby's a certain tree trunk
where I meet my babe, Danielle.
She sent a message with a finch
that I go fly to hell.

The hot tub has traumatised her
I'll miss her cute wing-span.
How many more chicks will flit.
I must concoct a plan…

I'll call a special meeting
of herons and other birds
near Dunnes Stores on Friday night
and confront those human nerds.

A real hip biker-bird,
I'll wear my leather jacket.
Have lots of beers with the gang.
Squawk up quite a racket.

Then full of booze, we'll cross the Suir
and without any remorse,
hover just above the tub
and let Nature take its course.

Mary O'Gorman
Waiting at the Gate
for Sarah and Sammy-Jo

The girl calls across fields
to where manes sway and tails flick
at deepening dusk in Tannersrath.

The bay mare lifts her head.
Begins to trot, to canter
till she gallops alone

by pools and paths and gaps
past hedges full of folded wings
and trees just touched by blossom.

The girl stands still at the gate
as hooves pull on the suck of mud,
first like distant drumming,

at the last gap like thunder –
with whinny and
a glimpse of blaze,

the mare bursts from shadows,
eyes dark with gladness.
Nuzzles the outstretched hand.

Sam Greene
First Date

It was just before the inter. cert. exams in 1979. As if life was not filled with enough complications, in the form of studying, spots, and peer pressurised drug taking. Women, or the lack of, were added to the equation. My parents house in Pond Road was used more often than not as a study area for me and my mates, Barry and Dave. Not because it was a big old Georgian building with lots of rooms to create an ambience conducive to learning, but for a number of other more important reasons altogether. Firstly, my bedroom window overlooked the beach, which in itself gave me and the lads an education that Frank Hall would never have approved of in the Irish cinema at the time. Secondly, the huge open fireplace in the bedroom afforded the lads the privilege of lying in the grate and blowing the smoke from all kinds of funky fags up the chimney. This was essential in getting stoned undetected, bearing in mind that there was no better smoke detector than my mother's nose. The third and most important of all, was the fact that the house itself was located en route to the Stella Maris Girls' School at the top of Pond Road. Ever since we had discovered the pleasures of girls, via imported magazines and the odd play for today on BBC 2, it became our life's obsession to get one or two each. As we all attended a 'Boys only' school, talking to women was the hardest thing in the world to do. They never responded well to our free flowing use of the four letter word. They were never interested in talking about the things that we wanted to talk about. They cared little about football and lighting fires. We researched women by reading our sisters' magazines. If there was a degree course available on how to make housework sexy, we would have graduated with flying colours, courtesy of 'Cosmopolitan'.

That day, we had decided to study English. We always decided to study English when we smoked our herbs. It sort of flowed much easier. We made excuses for this habit relying on the fact that most of the great poets of the world used substances to create great poetry. We could not prove this at all we merely relied upon what the drug pushers had told us at the time. We thought we were better than Jim Morrison and, as such, modified the words to some of his greatest songs. For example, 'Roadhouse Blues' went from 'Go in to the roadhouse gonna have a re-all———-good time', to 'Goin' down to Londis, gonna have to ste-all——

—-some sweets. 'Come on baby light my fire', was changed to something that would still infringe the obscenity laws of the land even today so I will not go there.

As Barry lay in the grate with a mushroom cloud of smoke emanating from his orifice, he began to wax lyrical. *"I wandered lonely as a cloud"*.

"High above Stella Maris's showers", offered Dave from his reclined position on the bed. They both looked at me for a follow on. I resorted to the original.

"When all at once I saw a crowd", I expected to receive a blow to the head for being too conservative. Dave was too quick. He had the last line made up before he even started.

"Show us yours and we'll show you ours", he cackled. Barry nearly choked and banged his head on the top of the fireplace as he tried to sit up properly. The effects of the imbibement made everything seem twice as funny as usual. My standard offering to the hilarious poem prevented me from joining in the laugh-a-thon. Instead, I noticed the time and brought the proceedings to a sharp halt.

"Lads", I hissed. "It's five to four." Without hesitation, they placed the speakers from the stereo system on the window sill of the bedroom facing out towards the road. Four minutes to four and the window was wide open. Three minutes to, and side two of 'Deep Purple, Made in Japan', was being cued up on the turntable. Barry hung out of the bedroom window with his binoculars trained on the school gates. We sat in silence. No point in starting too soon. We would get more attention from blaring 'Smoke on the water' than 'Black Knight'. Two minutes to go and Dave was holding Barry's legs to stop him from falling from the window ledge while I held the needle above the record. We all remained perfectly still as we waited for the stroke of four o' clock. Sweat beads appeared on my forehead as I watched the disc spinning at thirty-three and a third revolutions per minute. The centre of the record was purple with a big white 'P' on it. I was getting hypnotised by the effect. We waited with bated breath. Four o'clock, Barry waved the signal, I dropped the needle. The three of us crouched on the bed beneath the window, peeping over the window sill. Ritchie Blackmore gave that familiar guitar intro, with all the stops and starts for dramatic effect. Our hearts, well mine anyway, beat in time to the music. The crowd cheered in anticipation of the live performance. The sound from the speakers buzzed through our heads as we waited for the 'Stella' girls to appear. In the days before video and satellite television, this was as good as it got. We watched as the first years went past. I kept my hand on the volume knob ready to whack it up to the max. no point in wasting good sounds on the juniors.

"Here we go", whispered Barry as he spotted the particular gang of three fifth years at the school gates. "Cue the record again, it's nearly over", he hissed at me. It killed me to have to leave my vantage point at the window at a time when Sharon Casey was coming into view. She was gorgeous. Seventeen years old and we all fancied her. We heard stories that she only went out with men with cars. She only went out with married men, she only dated millionaires. We were not worthy of looking at her head on. God, here she comes. Cue record, volume max, back to the window. Sharon and her two friends drew nearer. They did their usual girlie thing of laughing and talking as they walked. I'm sure they were talking about us. Sure we were the only lads worth talking about ever since the last batch of leaving certificate students headed off to Dublin or London in search of work. One day, we knew that we would be heading off too, so we reckond that these girls had better make the most of us while they had the chance. If they missed their opportunity they would live in regret forever, especially as they stood around at the Lisdoonvarna festival, trying to bag a young farmer. The sound from the stereo drowned out my thoughts. I could only look. I needed reassurance.

"Are they lookin' up?" I asked, even though I could see for myself.

"Not yet", whispered Barry. "I think they need a little extra." With that he leaped up off the bed and in the process sent the speaker flying through the window on to the flower bed below. This in turn pulled the stereo from the table and scratched the shite out of my older brother's album. Barry scarpered out of the room like he was possessed by demons.

"They're lookin up now", said Dave as he remained in his original position. "Laughin' their kecks off so they are". He didn't have to tell me that as I was standing in the window in full view of the most wanted. At that point I knew that I was a dead man. My brother was goin' t'kill me because his prized record was sand papered. The best bird in Tramore had just decided that I was the funniest thing since her oulfella got fined as a 'found on' in Connolly's bar during the holy hour. But, much worse, I could see Barry, with his dope-fuelled ego, was now down in the garden drawing attention to himself.. "Hey girls", shouted Barry from the garden below. "That new Floyd album is bleedin' rapid. It blows the speakers off the wall. Yis should come in an' listen to it." I couldn't believe my ears let alone my eyes when the girls entered the garden. Sharon Casey was in my garden. It was a dream. It was a nightmare. It seemed as if they moved in slow motion while I moved at high speed, clearing week old underpants and socks from the bedroom floor. I could hear them on the stairs now. Getting closer by the second. I shook the talcum powder around the room and waved my arms about wildly to make it settle down faster. The heady smell of sweaty jockeys filled the air. I could hear Barry extolling the virtues of Floyd's 'Wish You Were Here'. They came closer. I could hear them giggling outside the door. My heart thumped. The door opened. They entered. Six of us stood in the bedroom. There was silence. The girls shifted closer together. I'm goin' home", announced Dave as he slithered off the bed and exited followed by Barry. Sharon's two friends also made a hasty exit, which left just me and Sharon. Sweat appeared all over my body to which the cloud of talcum powder seemed to be attracted. I began to turn white. She stood between me and the door. I wanted to run for it. I mopped my sweating brow with the collection of underwear that I still had gripped in my hand. She moved closer to me. I fell backwards on to the bed. "I've got something for you," she said seductively. I leaned backwards and heard the crack of another 'Deep Purple' album being shattered beneath my weight. "You have?" I replied as seductively as a lettuce leaf drenched in olive oil. "Oh yes," she said slowly as she returned my wayward loudspeaker with the precision of a Jewish circumsiser. "And if you don't stop harassing me and my mates every time you see us," she roared, "I'll come back and finish the job." At least that's what I think she said. I was too busy nursing my damaged pride to really be listening. The door slammed as she left. After that experience, what is a young man supposed to do? Lie of course.

When I saw my mates again, I still had a strange 'John Wayne' type way of walking. The pain she had inflicted upon my boyhood/manhood was still evident. All I could say was: *"Me an' Sharon. My bedroom. First date. I was great."* That was enough to ruin the reputation of young Sharon, whereas of course I was hailed as a hero. The stud of Stella. I wondered why I never managed to get a girlfriend from that school after that.

Emir Kelly
Silk Gown

With time and patience, the mulberry leaf becomes a silk gown. (Oriental Proverb)

Wayne Dyer in Wisdom of the Ages
says he thinks of his children
as silk gowns in the making
as I do mine
revelling in each stage of their transformation.

Why then be critical of my own metamorphosis
Judging the worm-eaten leaves
the length of time cocoon
the tangled knots
the cut
the dye
the style
the workmanship
and ultimately
will it fit me
will I fit it.

Emir Kelly
Restoration
for Ruth Byrne

Like the kitchen table
I was scarred, dinted, dulled,
life's wear and tear etched deep
into a once polished surface,
shrouded with stiff linen from view
sadly tracing the marks when alone.

Slowly fine sandpaper lifts old laquer,
and smooths soft pine,
revealing the pale beauty of now exposed grain,
patient work builds up a protective lustre
that allows its honeyed soul shine through,
and I'm reflected in its glow.

20

Emir Kelly
Holy Cairn

If things were good or bad
choice would be easy
but black and white are rubbed
to dingy grey and now
you walk a dark and empty land
where memory ploughs sharp
stones of joy, betrayal.

Allow the frost to powder rigid clods
and winter sun to sweeten broken clay
Pick up each stone and make a holy cairn
to mark the seeds you choose to plant today.

Emir Kelly
Embrace the Wind

Embrace the wind I'm told.
Me, reared on names like
shiver the win
cold creature
hot house flower
the standing joke being
it would take a general anaesthetic
to remove my cardigan.
Still, embrace the wind
has a majestic ring to it
encompassing health, freedom, exuberance.
Tomorrow I'll embrace the wind
if it's a nice day.

22

Noel Greaney

Handnotes

for Jack Ryan

Years of toil
Hard work
Powerful hands
Glide
Like a ballet dancer
Pirouetting across the stage
Like a skater on ice
Gliding
Up and down
The neck of the fiddle.
Tunes
As sweet as ripened apples
Pour forth
Unending
Yes
They're your hands
Your tunes
Only you
Can play them
With the magical
Precision of the
Master craftsman
Of notes.

23

Noel Greaney
Serendipity

Dip in its serenity
Intrepid deity
Reside inside
Enter
Tense tired spent
Rise
Respited.

24

Noel Greaney
The Child Within

The little girl inside me
Wants to come out
Come out
Scream and shout
At my mother
My father
My brother
My sister.

I've been a Mum
To one and all
Now I want the little girl
To be mothered
By myself
By one and all.

A ribbon for my hair
A bow for my shoe
That's all I ever wanted
To be mothered
By you my Mother.

Where did the child stop
Parent begin
Where did the parent stop
Child begin
Boundaries obliterated
Bombed from on high
By you
Gone was the little girl.

Boundaries will be rebuilt
Fences re-erected
The bombardment will stop
The little girl will return
To be spoiled
With ribbons laces and bows
By me
By the mother I've become.

Noel Greaney

Pope Jacinta Patricia II

The 'oul bag
Imagine not allowing
Men become priests.
Does she not see
Down the road she's
Going to need us men.
Why shut us out?

Them with their
Designer robes –
Gucci, Versace
And the like
. Gold and silver jewellery
With matching accessories
Poncing around in their fine carriages.

Just because Jesus
Was a women –
And some beauty at that –
They get all the breaks.
Why! Even abortion
It's solely the choice of the woman
We have no say
We can't even mention
Vasectomy
Without causing a flurry

Are we eternally destined
To be the footmen of God?
Always the bestmen
Never the grooms
Yes
As long as Jacinta
Is at the helm.

Shauna McGarry-Egan
Serendipity

I remember coming back from Sligo during February school break. Approaching the house, it was very dark but I remember seeing lights in the trees behind my home at Russelstown Wood. Coming up the hill I could not fathom out the lights. The thought of an alien spaceship shot through my mind, As I opened the car I heard loud sounds of sawing wood. What I had dreaded for years was happening.

The part of the wood that encircled the house, which had protected us from cold north winds, which had provided a tree house and playing area for my children, was being cut down.

For weeks I watched in the mornings and evenings, before and after work, as the wood disappeared and I felt sorrow at its departure.

At the end of March, I felt hope. There was much more light at the gable end of the house. I could see shadows of morning and evening. I had never seen the sky from that side of the house before and there were small joys like the washing on the line drying faster.

With the extra light plants that had never been there before began to grow. In April, there were woodland flowers popping up and blooming. Carpets of bluebells and red campion and butter bur. Before this these plants only grew at the edge of the forest.

During the following July and August I often sat on one of the tree stumps, supported by a stretch of bark that the fellers had not completely taken away. The bareness had gone. There was so much light and growth. It had become a magical place. As I looked around me I saw that some of the roots had become completely dug up with the exertion of the huge saws. These roots had magical shapes, one reminded me of a witch's head with scrawny hair. Another root had the shape of a rhino.

In among the the tangle of abandoned roots were occasional large stones, erratics, some of these had beautiful shapes, some very smooth having been protected from the wind and rain by the trees over time. The stones were of granite and red sandstone and the odd bit of limestone.

When I breakfasted there in late August in that magical place I could see the withering tall spikes of the once beautiful purple foxglove. There were oceans of ferns and tall grasses all over the place, profuse because of the tropical Summer.

It was and is a serendipitous place.

David Power
Original Sin in Donaskeigh

Sharp, severe and sixty – she stood
Ramrod straight before us with grey bun
Of hair resting on canary yellow jacket;
Three shiny buttons glittered in the glare
Of winter fire. She looked at me
With cold grey eyes waving a long cane
To heighten her cruel intent. "You," she intoned,
"What are the effects of Original Sin?"
The God of love was never born
In the hearts of fourth class minds;
The cruel God of Isaac and Jacob
Failed to rally to my fervent prayer.
"It weakens the wi-will", I stuttered;
Two more to go – pray God I get them right.
"Darkens the understanding" – "Yes", she urged;
Only one more to go. The Red Sea closed
Before me, and my chariots of thought
Were drowned with my panic
"and leaves us in a strong inclination
To DARKNESS". Wrong! Oh my God!
The avenging goddess waved her stick
Like Aaron's rod. My tears gushed forth
Like water from the rock.
"A strong inclination to EVIL", she screamed.
Oh, slave and stooge to Eve's first folly,
Her stupid sin had now damned me.
O Jesebel, you wretched woman, may the dogs
Eat you up in the streets today.
The God of love, once more crucified.
My hands and feet showed the marks of Cain.

David Power
Icarian Limits

Soft zephyrs caressing a vast expanse
Of ocean deep, rolling gently beneath them
Graded swells to tune of Neptune's lyre
Hippotades, awake from faery spell, blows loud
Raising the crest of foamy waves;
See ocean's loss in the vapoured mists arise,
Ascend the humid air of elevated transport
Careering wildly in the clouded majesty;
Up. Up above the limestone cliffs of Clare,
Still up beyond Icarian limits toward
The sun of Artic cold – tiny droplets
Growing larger like Titan's brood
Cool, condense and plunge down the
Wax wing fall to wooded glens below.

30

David Power
Life

I wonder why I sometimes rage
'Gainst the cryptic clues of God's design,
Puzzle out each complex sign,
Balance, check and sometimes gauge
Why life is like a sterile cage;
Why each one beams his eye on mine
Speaks with tongue of sparkling wine
As if my wounds he would assuage.
When mine eyes are unaware –
Epee, dagger, cutlass, sword – yet he'll fawn
Though each sharp blade is naked there.
I trust in God but not in man
A hypocrite since Time began.

David Power
The Big House

Trench-coated 'gainst the October rain
A single mind gropes towards release in action;
The five move stealthily past Tubrid
Up the minister's hill;
Reconnaissance and preparatory work complete;
Stage two awaits unfolding;
The big house, that was wont to cast
Its ascendant eye on Ceitinn,
Hosts anarchy tonight.
A turmoil of sparks wrapped in the dull
Grey smoke illuminate the night
As the roof crashes to polished floors below;
The charred oak beams-gaunt, aloft, alight,
Hiss to a ceaseless pattern of dancing tears
Weeping for a troubled night of Ireland's dream;
Wine cellar, books, big house, all consumed,
Fell victim to a mindless philosophy;
A Georgian discipline lies in ruins;
A theme of destruction complete.

Derbhile Dromey
Extract from her novel 'Athalie'

Their house was big and white, one of the biggest in the village near Rennes where their father was a doctor. The surgery was attached to the side of the house. Their mother helped there sometimes, but mostly, she was in the kitchen, a vital presence, greeting Miriam and Claudine when they returned home from school with gauffres, the Breton specialty of sweet sticky bread covered in chocolate. Miriam always ate hers with relish, Claudine usually slipped the remainder of her slice into Miriam's hand when their mother, Colette, wasn't looking.

Colette died suddenly, shortly after Claudine's confirmation. Their father, Maurice, insisted that they should have new dresses for the funeral. Otherwise he seemed to forget they were there, as he sorted out funeral arrangements, and the disposal of Colette's clothes.
Claudine stood quietly beside her father at the funeral, her fair hair shining. She had brushed Miriam's hair earlier but it still stuck out in dark chunks. Like her mother's.
Claudine could see Miriam's eyes brimming with tears. Of course, she was only nine, she couldn't understand the importance of maintaining composure in public. Their father would not be happy. She squeezed Miriam's hand, feeling grown up, although she was only three years older.

The day was confusing for Miriam. There were a lot of people in the house, talking in low voices. She wanted her mother. Claudine was helping Aunt Daphne pour tea.
Later, Claudine came to where she sat with her teddy bear.
"It's time for bed, Miriam," she said gently.
"I'm scared, Claudine. Maybe there are monsters, the ones who took Mummy away."
"Don't be silly. I'll come with you."
She took Miriam's hand and they went upstairs. Miriam got into bed. Claudine said she would be back to read to her. Claudine had a lovely nightdress that Mummy had given her for her confirmation.
Instead of reading to her, Claudine crawled into bed beside her. When Miriam turned around, she saw that Claudine was crying. Miriam began

33

to cry too, and clung to Claudine. Their tears fell on each other's shoulders.

When Miriam woke up the next day, Claudine was already up. She was making breakfast for them all.

At twelve, Claudine had virtually taken over the running of the house. She could see that this was what her father expected of her. She cooked, cleaned and washed, helped by a housekeeper who came in while Miriam and Claudine attended their convent in Rennes. Claudine knew that her father wanted neatly pressed shirts, dinner at seven, the front pew at Mass, and neatly dressed, softly spoken daughters. She ensured that that was what he got.

Miriam gradually began to recover her happy-go-lucky nature. At weekends, while Claudine stayed at home and studied or did housework, Miriam played with her friends by the river in summer, and in various houses in winter. More often than not, a boiled sweet was lodged in her cheek, but she still found room for the dinners Claudine prepared. At school, giggling and passing secret notes to her friends held more appeal for her than studying. She was always being compared to Claudine. But Miriam didn't mind. Claudine was always on hand to help her with maths homework, ensure that her uniform was clean and that she got to school on time.

The September evening still retained the warmth of summer. Claudine was glad the bus had been on time today. She was going to make her father's favourite chicken dish. She hoped Father would not be delayed at the surgery. In her mind, she ran over what she would say to him. Her stomach knotted. It had to go right later.

Miriam noticed Claudine's hand tremble as she poured water into Father's glass. She had been very quiet on the bus on the way home.
She lifted the fork to her mouth, and then put it back down.
"Father, there is something I wish to discuss with you."
"Yes?" He looked impatient.
"It's about my plans for next year." Claudine's voice was low.
"I'm glad to see you're thinking about your future, Claudine. I have, in fact, also been thinking about this. I was going to show you these at the weekend. I'll just go to my study and get them."

Claudine mashed her potatoes slowly, concentrating on her plate. She thought of the prospectus, hidden upstairs in her top drawers. Perhaps her father had the same one. Her eyes were closed.

Maurice came back in.

"I took the liberty of getting you these. They provide excellent courses." Claudine opened her eyes. She stared at the two booklets. The letters danced in front of her eyes. Rennes Commercial College.

"There are courses in bookkeeping, secretarial skills. I thought you might also like to combine it with a cookery course."

"But, Father, I had something rather different in mind."

She did her best to keep her voice steady. She mustn't let it slip away now.

"And what was that exactly."

Maurice's voice was calm, but Miriam could hear the vibrations in it. Claudine cleared her throat.

"There are several courses I am interested in at the University of Rennes, in Mathematics and the liberal arts."

"And what would you do with that? Teach?" The dismissiveness in his voice was unmistakeable. Miriam's eyes were round.

"No." Claudine's voice was almost a whisper. "I want to become a professor of Mathematics."

"I think it's important to be realistic Claudine. University is not a suitable option for a woman like you."

"It's 1930, Father. Women go to university."

Miriam's jaw dropped. Claudine was never cheeky with her father. That was usually Miriam's bailiwick.

Maurice's face was stern. It was unlike Claudine to have silly flights of fancy.

"Perhaps for some women, who need to earn their livings. But you will marry, and have children. You will, of course, need to earn money until that date. These courses will equip you with the skills you need."

"As you wish, Father," Claudine said, lowering her head.

"Why did you give in to him like that," Miriam blurted, as Claudine washed the dishes. Miriam was drying. Claudine watched her carefully to ensure she dried everything thoroughly.

"He pays the fees," she said.

"What if you didn't have to pay fees."

"Don't be silly, Miriam. Everyone pays fees."

"M. Millet's son got a scholarship. Maybe you could get one. There might be a Maths scholarship."

Miriam hopped up and down on one leg.

"Miriam, please put that tea-cup down. You'll break it."

"Talk to Monsieur Aurel, Claudine. He'll help you."

"I'll think about it. Now please finish drying. It's almost time for prayers."

The Maths class was almost over. Claudine put her protractor and compass in her geometry set.

Monsieur Aurel was cleaning the blackboard as Claudine approached.

"Excuse me, Sir."

Monsieur Aurel turned around. Claudine stood, twisting her hands anxiously.

"Claudine, what can I do for you?"

Claudine looked around the classroom to ensure that everyone was gone.

"I would like to enquire about the possibility of Maths scholarships to the University of Rennes."

The words came out in a rush.

"I see. Surely your father would…"

"I would like to surprise him."

"Oh." He looked a little startled. "I'll look into it for you, Mademoiselle. I'll let you know by the end of the week."

M. Aurel could see quite clearly what the situation was. She was a bright girl, the only one in the school at present with any kind of aptitude. It would be a pity if that went to waste.

Claudine's Maths book was open, but for once, Claudine wasn't concentrating on it. She was studying the contents of the envelope M. Aurel had given her. All the details were there. She knew exactly what she had to do. Carefully, she put the envelope into her top drawer, next to the prospectus. She tried to return to her work. But nothing would come to her. She stared at the blank sheet of paper in front of her. Suddenly she picked up her pen. Over and over again she wrote, Dr. Claudine Brillon, Professor Claudine Brillon. Claudine Brillon, Professor of Mathematics. Then she tore out the sheet of paper and threw it in the wastepaper basket. There was no time for this idle dreaming; she was being as frivolous as Miriam and her friends now.

Claudine had always spent longer at her homework than Miriam. But even Miriam had never seen Claudine study so hard. Every night, Claudine's light stayed on in her room past midnight. Miriam heard girls on the bus laughing about her and calling her a swot. It was strange the way she had no friends, and even stranger that she never seemed to need any. Claudine studied while the other girls dreamed of the end of year dance, the boys they would meet, the dresses they would wear.

The results of Claudine's baccalaureate exams were the highest in the school's history. Miriam knew that she would be compared to Claudine even more now for the next three years, especially since she was moving into the senior school next year. But she didn't care. It meant that Claudine would be eligible to sit the scholarship exam at the end of August.

The summer was hot and sticky. The village was near the sea, but had no beach. So Miriam and her friends spent the summer by the river. Her father was working, and Claudine was studying, so she felt quite free. But still she felt anxious about Claudine as the day of the exam approached.

Claudine told Maurice that she wanted to spend a day in Rennes, orienting herself with the commercial college and maybe meeting some of the staff. She would be home in time to cook dinner.

The manila envelope arrived at the beginning of September. Claudine was able to intercept it as she collected her father's post. Miriam saw her go up to her room with it, as she picked her swimming costume out of the washbasket to take to the river. By the time Miriam was ready to go, Claudine still hadn't come out of her room.

The river wasn't as much fun as usual that day. Miriam decided to come home early to see if Claudine was all right.
She was on the phone when Miriam came in.
"I see...yes...I understand. Thank you."

She put down the receiver. Her face was very pale, her eyes gazed past Miriam as she went upstairs.

The door of her room was still closed. Miriam decided to start dinner. She liked cooking, in fact she suspected she liked it more than Claudine did.

"Where's Claudine," Maurice asked, mopping his forehead as he sat down for dinner.

"She has a headache."

"Perhaps if she took a little more sun, she would feel better. She's looking very peaky, spending all day in her room with those books of hers."

"I'm sure she'll be fine tomorrow, Father."

Miriam took a tray upstairs, deciding to brave Claudine's closed door. Claudine didn't say anything, so Miriam opened the door. Claudine sat at her desk, sharpening a pencil. She had sharpened all her pencils, the shavings were in a neat pile beside the sheet of paper with the university letterhead.

Claudine turned.

"Thank you Miriam, I'm not hungry."

"You didn't get it?"

Claudine handed Miriam the letter. Miriam scanned it. "Regret to inform you….very close competition…wish you luck in your studies."

"It was a man. He beat me by a point." Her voice was expressionless. "They rang to congratulate me and said they looked forward to seeing me in October."

She gave a mirthless laugh.

Miriam ran over to her, wanting to hug her. Claudine turned away.

"Miriam, I'd rather be alone now, if you don't mind. Thank you for your sympathy."

Later, for the second time in her life, Miriam heard the sound of Claudine's sobs, raw and heavy.

Paddy Phelan
Confessions of Celia

Now my Bertie surely looks the part
When he jogs ver-ti-call-y,
But you should see him horizontal
When he jogs on me.

He really takes my breath away,
He is so fit and hard;
But if I mention marriage
He turns into lard.

Once I said I'd write a book,
(This was long before Cecelia)
But I dropped it like a roasted spud,
Sure he'd lost the rag completely.

He told me if I did the dirt,
That I'd find him lean and mean,
I'd be banished from the inner courts,
And end like Terry Keane!

We had many trips around the world,
My Bertie bold and I,
But one occasion was so sweet,
I near o'erflowed with joy.

When they called me Señora 'Hearne
Way down in Mexico,
It made me part of Bertie,
And Oh! I loved him so!

I know he didn't hold my hand,
Like the other leader,
But then she was his wifey wife,
And I was Bertie's Celia.

Now my lover he was very mad,
When the plane it wouldn't fly,
And he said to me "dear Celia,
We will fix this bye and bye.

I'll get a sexy new machine,
With a well sprung double bed,
(He's such a cuddly loving man
Such things get in his head).

And then the Dail can fume and fart,
As we ride one mile high,
And we'll be members of that club,
My Celia, you and I!

And if they quiz me in the Dail,
'Bout the cost and all that crack,
I will play handball with them,
Against a big hay stack."

Now Bertie often told me:
"You'r feelings must be masked,
And you answer every question
Except the one you're asked.

If they ask about Shannon and the Yanks,
You tell them 'bout their jobs,
And as for dem protesters,
They're just a crowd of yobs."

Now Bertie did confide in me:
"I don't know what to do,
Will I follow the Bush fire
Or the Franco-German two?

The Yanks were always good to us,
Put bobs on bedside lockers;
And Europe built us brand new roads,
Gave the farmers golden knockers."

I told him to stay neutral,
And have the best of both,
"And don't be heeding people
Accusing you of sloth."

He turned then and said to me:
"You know I love you, dear,
And I love Miriam as well,
You've made my case quite clear.

You two have done so much for me,
I have to back you both,
And to hell with all those people,
Accusing me of sloth!"

When I pointed out the war I meant
Was Saddam versus Bush,
(I was crying now with temper)
And he said "my Celia, hush,

I know you're worried 'bout the war,
And all those people dyin',
Here's my hankie for you now,
I hate to see your cryin'."

And then Joe Higgins thinks it's hard
An answer to extract ———
If Bertie he was neutered,
He'd be neutral, that's a fact.

Paddy Phelan
Bertiespeak

Now de 'lection it is over
And we are back in power,
All de people love us
Dey dont trust dat other shower.

I gave dem lots of promises
I ran in and out of town
And I warned all me drivers
Dont knock anybody down.

Dey say I have charisma
And Haughey says I'm clever,
I know I'm touchy-feely,
De cuddliest Taoiseach ever.

Das why de people vote for me,
And believe me all the time,
Even when the things I say
Have no reason or no rime.

I've a native way of speakin'
And a different words a usin'
Dat may not be convincin'
But tis sure as hell confusin'.

Sometimes I gets mixed up meself,
But I never do let on
Before de hacks can work it out
De problem is long gone.

De secret is keep talking
And saying dis and dat
And den before dey know it
Dey're into a cocked hat.

Dey're saying know dat Rabbit,
Is a smarter man dan me,
But when de fur is flying
What will dey say, hee! hee!

But I will not kill off Rabbit,
I'll just trap him in my stare,
And use me Dublin lingo
To leave his skin quite bare.

And if dat don't fix him
And he takes me to a crunch,
I wont like to have to do it
But I'll use me rabbit punch.

And as far as Enda Kenny,
Dat man is so polite
When you listen to him talkin'
'twould nearly make you –ah- white!

Dey do be on about me Bowl
And de way it got bowled over.
I taut twould be me monument
When I go out to clover.

De hole ting went against me,
Sure I met meself at Croker,
I was much too clever for meself
I'm such an able broker!

I taut we'd pull de World Cup
Between de harp and kilt,
Sure we showed em all de pitches
'Wid no bit of concrete spilt.

43

Now when you come to Dublin,
You can look at Bertie's Spike;
And Harney & McDowell
Can go and take a hike!

Dem two, dey always shag me up,
With deir hiperbole,
Mary so contrary
And yer man stuck up his —a- pole.

McDowell and O'Connell
Dey are arguing the toss
About who runs de country
Dont dey know dat I'm de boss?

Sure the only problem dat I have
Is not 'bout kissing rings,
Tis more bout kissing Celia
And de constant song she sings.

Miriam has her own song:
"Dis ring stay put on me!"
While Celia keeps nagging:
"I gives you more dan she!"

'Twas very true for Albert:
"Sure das the way with wimmin!",
They're lucky I m not Taliban
I'd give them both a trimmin'.

Jenni Rope
Sandymount Strand

Grey pastel purple hues
smudged with morning sky
blend along the bay
over the sands
to the tips of the land.

Puddles of sea, puddles of sand
and a grey stone wall
frame the chalky drawing from disturbance
as the peace stretches past the horizon.

At dusk it is a dome.
Wave imprinted sand.
The chimney stack smoke
creating clouds, sealing us in.
The light bends.

At night there is neither bay nor sea
save its sound.
Just sodium pearls
draped in rows
hanging on the darkness.

Jenni Rope
The Rhinoceros
Written in Jabalpur Wildlife Park, India.

I've just seen a cube in the garden!
A cube in the garden outside.
Well, four grey cubes if you'll pardon –
I'm solo, I'm without a guide.

The four cubes fuse and they harden
into rhinoceros hide.
It's munching green strips in the garden
and I click on my camera with pride.

46

Jenni Rope
Mint

For my Dadcu*

I was in the garden.
The warm yellow sun shone
on fat bees humming in the lavender.
Our dogs were barking in the distance,
rolling round in their green happiness.
I bent to smell the mint.

I was struck!
Left inwardly staggering.
Knocked backwards by a forgotten memory –
all beige and Formica.
An engraved tin teapot and flat cap.
Brown paper bags and jam jars stuffed with dried
mint,
liver spot hands pulling the brittle stalks clean.

Now he is
as the rest of the dead were
on that final day.
A black stone, an empty chair.
He is gone! He is gone!

Yet, the thorns of grief are,
eventually,
blanketed by the soft moss of remembrance,
and the breach feels more like a Saturday noon
when I'd wait for his return
ready to help with the mint.

* *Dadcu –Welsh for Grandfather.*

Jenni Rope
4 A.M.

Comfy fitted zeds
lying tessellate
rise and fall to the rhythm of breath.
Deep, dark, warm.
Drowsy bodies sink deeper into sleep.

As she stirs, he readjusts their fitting
moving straying hair from the snug of the neck.
Reconnected
circuit complete
comfort flows through them once more.

Sleep is a weight drawing them down.
A thick duvet cushions their slide
further and further
into delicious sub-consciousness
and the night drifts on.

48

Majella Whelan
Extract from the novel 'Prelude', Chapter 11

Streetlights hung suspended against the dark sky, emitting an electric orange glare that lent an illusion of warmth to slick city streets and outshone the feeble rays cast forth by countless cars crawling beneath them like insects with feverishly burning eyes. Judith opened her window a little, welcoming the blast of misty air that clung in droplets to her skin and hair and refreshed the stale, smoky atmosphere of the car. It was still pitch dark when she reached the staff car-park. She watched the surreal flow of faceless, hooded students filing up the schoolyard under a nocturnal sky, feeling as though she was part of a scene from some sci-fi movie. As she joined the throng of students making their way towards the main entrance, the cold wind seeped through the thin fabric of her raincoat and squeezed her body in its icy grip.

Initially, Judith took comfort in the contrasting warmth of the centrally-heated school building, but mid-way into the second class period the cloying atmosphere of the classroom made her feel ill again. Loud voices of protest emerged from the incredulous students seated before her in their coats, at her suggestion that they open the windows. "Jesus Miss, are ye mad? We'll perish!" She was left with no alternative therefore, but to suffer the intensity of the many bodies packed tightly into the small, over-heated music room. She felt the blood drain from her face at one point during the lesson and realized with panic that she was close to fainting. The absolutely mortifying possibility of falling to the floor in a crumpled heap at the top of the room was unthinkable and so Judith instructed the students to carry on with their exercise while she fetched something from the staff-room.

The corridor reeled in and out of focus as she staggered along its length in the direction of the bathroom and she bolted through the door just in time. She hung over the toilet bowl and held her hair back from her face while she gagged painfully although there was nothing inside of her. Her insides felt as though they were being twisted tight inside an iron fist and the cramps sent Judith to her knees where she continued to heave and retch emptily for a couple of minutes that felt like forever. She took a small sip of water from the faucet and washed her face. Leaning her forehead against the cold mirror, she tried to decide what to do next. She could not return to the stultifying confines of the music room even though she could hear the raucous talk and loud laughter of her unsupervised charges echoing around the corridor and knew that her absence would have been detected almost immediately by the teachers at either side of her room.

Judith looked at her reflection in the mirror and a stranger returned her gaze. She hardly recognised herself in the image of the wretched looking creature with ghostly pale skin, apart from the dark rings that encircled her hollow eyes. As she closed the bathroom door behind her, she encountered Mr. Byrne, the principal, making his way along the corridor towards her. Her heart sank and she reddened under his gaze, feeling like a student caught mitching.

"Judith! How are you?" he greeted her with a friendly smile as he approached.

"Good morning, Mr. Byrne", Judith mumbled, "I was just..." He cut off her explanation with a wave of his hand as he peered at her, scrutinising the deathly pallor of her complexion.

"Goodness Judith, you don't look well at all. Are you all right?" he inquired.

"Ah sure, I must be coming down with a cold or something. I'll be grand."

"You should be at home tucked up in your bed by the look of you", he admonished, "there are no medals for martyrdom being given out by the Minister for Education, you know! Far from it!" Mr. Byrne chuckled at his wit and Judith smiled weakly.

"Look Judith, why don't you go on home and I'll get the rest of your classes sorted out?"

"Ah no, Mr. Byrne, honestly", she assured him, trying her best to look sprightly as they walked back along the corridor together.

"No, go on", he urged, "go away and mind yourself. You look completely done in and anyway, today's only a half-day so it won't create much of an upheaval. Stay in bed for the week-end. You don't want to be sick for the whole of mid-term."

"Well...all right then. Thanks very much, Mr. Byrne. Are you sure I'm not putting you out though?"

"Nonsense." He waved away Judith's concern with another expansive sweep of his hand before entering Judith's classroom.

"Quiet, you lot!" he roared with such ferocity that even Judith almost jumped out of her skin. She entered the cowed silence of the room and quickly grabbed her coat and brief-case while Mr. Byrne launched into a lecture about how he would "have expected a bit more cop-on from a group of Junior Cert. students..." Judith nodded gratefully to him as she left and he grinned at her, rolling his eyes in exaggerated fashion from his position behind the pupils at the back of the room.

She felt decidedly improved upon leaving the school building and was touched by Mr. Byrne's act of kindness. It was wonderful to be released unexpectedly from her duties although Judith had no idea what she would do with herself for the rest of the day, let alone the following week's mid-term break. It was still only half-past ten and she just couldn't face the prospect of returning to her grim bed-sit. She switched on the ignition and lit a cigarette before pulling out the school gate pondering the problem of how she might fill her day. The street was deathly quiet. It seemed almost as if the external world had been shocked into silent submission by the numbing cold. Everybody was indoors, either at work, at school or at home, Judith assumed.

She noticed thin wisps of smoke drifting from the chimneys of some of the small terraced houses on the opposite side of the street, wondering briefly how much of the swirling fog into which it disappeared was smog. She checked for the third time that her head-lights were on as she sat waiting for the deserted traffic lights to change colour. She tried to imagine the possible scenes that lay behind the firmly closed wooden doors of the terraced houses and images of cosy domesticity conjured up in her mind of elderly men in carpet slippers, sitting by roaring fires while plump women hummed contentedly in kitchens enveloped by aromas of hearty meals being cooked for lunch. Perhaps a cat or shaggy dog lay curled in a snooze by the fire or small children sat on soft rugs, their faces illuminated by the neon glow of animated figures tumbling across television screens while tired mothers sat at kitchen tables drinking coffee and listening to Gerry Ryan on the radio.

For a brief moment, Judith longed to be a part of some such household, yet decided almost immediately that she would go out of her mind if she was required to spend her days cooking and cleaning in a house where she listened to the radio for company. It all seemed a bit pointless and trivial. Existence itself, in fact, presented itself to her as futile, not for the first time, on that February morning when the city lay wrapped in a blanket of freezing fog. She wondered despondently if there was actually a point to this hum-drum of forward marching through time that people adhered to as part of their rigid survival routine each day. What was the purpose, she wondered, of acknowledging and perhaps even embracing a day that brought everyone a step closer to an inevitable end? Why did nobody talk about the meaninglessness of it all? Did other people even

51

think like this or was she the only person who viewed life in this way? Had she somehow missed some important point that would have otherwise filled her days with determination and purpose?

Judith had no answers to the questions that her mind threw at her, like the quiz master in that "Brains Beat The Clock" T.V. show. Abruptly, she switched on the car radio, something she very rarely did, in order to hear what someone else's thoughts were on some matter of supposed significance. The mellow timbre of Gerry Ryan's voice filled the silence and Judith listened to his eloquent, heart-felt agreement with some caller that yes indeed, the university points system was putting almost insurmountable pressure on the country's young people and should certainly be revised and.... Judith switched off the radio again, preferring the sleepy silence of the car to a barrage of words being used vainly in an attempt to solve the insoluble ills of society. Did people not get it? she thought angrily. There was no point to eloquence because change happened slowly in spite of rather than because of it while people, in general, unwittingly hurtled along their own individual paths in life, laying track. She drove quickly past the three looming blocks of flats on her left, not wanting to have to look at their defiant grey mass, broken in places by balcony lines of stiff, multi-coloured clothing. She did not want to think about the huge number of people inside them, each caught up in his or her own silent, invisible existence.

Judith's heart started to pound as she caught sight of a small figure kneeling on the footpath outside the high brick wall that enclosed the community. She slowed to a crawl and watched the child. He was the same small boy who had been standing outside the school playing field the previous day. He was kneeling at the curbside, intent upon his task of shattering iced-over puddles of water with a stone. "What was he doing out here by himself?" she wondered. He could be knocked down, for heaven's sake, leaning out into the street like that. Dutifully, Judith stopped her car and opened the passenger door. The small boy looked up and squinted at her curiously through his spectacles. A stream of snot hung from each nostril, suspended mid-way between nose and mouth. She smiled tentatively and wondered whether he would allow her to wipe his nose. "Hello there. What are you doing out here all by yourself?" The child continued to stare silently at her. "Fuck off", he replied, his small face screwing up in a grimace of defiance. Judith stared back, incredulous that she had just witnessed such a profanity issued by such a small, high-pitched voice; the perfect pronunciation, the bland tonelessness in which such an evidently routine remark had been passed, shocked her. "Where's your Mammy?" she asked the boy, choosing to ignore his baffling greeting. "Should you be out here by yourself?" She watched the flicker of recognition cross his features.

"Mammy asleep, tired", he told her in a friendlier tone as he pointed beyond the wall with the small purple hand that held the stone.

"Well…I don't think she'd like you to be out here alone", Judith told him, wondering in her own mind what the hell kind of mother went to sleep while her small child played alone outside in the street?

"Look, why don't I drive you in home?" she suggested.

"Okay", the boy agreed, hopping quickly through the open car door.

"In the back", Judith ordered firmly, her heart suddenly soaring with pleasure as the boy obediently clambered across the gear stick and sat in the back seat staring up at her. She smiled at him and her chest ached upon noticing that his sneakered feet only reached to the edge of the seat. He was so tiny. Overcome by a desire to touch the child, she stretched her hand back and gave his knee a little pat. "Good fellow. Off we go then."

"Off we go then!" he echoed excitedly as Judith glanced in her rear-view mirror before pulling away from the curb. She drove slowly forward in first gear, searching for a suitable spot at which to execute a u-turn and drive the child back to his door. She noticed absently that there was nobody around, not even a dog.

53

Suddenly, Judith didn't want to bring the boy back inside the wall, to let himself in some door where his Mammy lay asleep inside. She did not want him to leave the back seat of her car, where he sat gazing contentedly out the window, looking so perfect back there right behind her.

"Will we get sweets?" she asked him without hesitation. The little boy's face creased into a smile as he raised his shoulders to his ears and clapped.

"Sweets! Sweets!" he shouted in reply, kicking his legs up and down against the seat.

"Okay then! Off we go for sweets!" Judith shouted and laughed, feeling triumphant and exhilarated as she stepped recklessly on the accelerator, feeling like a person does when they realize with relief that they have just turned the final bend on the roller coaster ride as her small red fiesta sped down a side street and out onto the intersecting main ring road.

John Fitzgerald
Graves and Gravel

A serpentine pathway meandering through
Lichen-encrusted tombs and sepulchres
Illegible etchings fragments of facts
Side by side in gentle repose

Wildly tilting headstones
Like forgotten teeth
Suggest in their jagged incongruity
The turbulence of interred restfulness

Fox and nature make their way
Where once churchgoers gathered
To regale and swap their way of life
And pray as one as one might pray

Battered belfry behind louvered doors
Pointing now as pointing then
To vaulting heavens universal hope
For mundane men and common folk

Pews of prayer segregated you
Tithes and privations uneasy sat
Man has dug the paupers grave
Egalitarian death if you could pay

Sermonised the chausubled priest
Font pulpit altar and grave
Ancestral tableau silenced now
Nightingales and pigeons coo

54

Walls of stone gates of steel
Fall and warp beneath the clock
Layers of verdigris and time
Supplant the suppliant now long gone

Arching yews with watchman's eyes
In search of steps that bend this way
For in the silence speaks decay
The pathos of the parting way

John Fitzgerald.
Indiscretion

I peeped into my bedroom,
And there they were inside.
Romping about beneath the moon,
Rolling from side to side.

They never saw my look of stealth,
As they thrashed with legs entwined.
The scurrilous pair were in their pelt,
Kama Sutra was trotting behind.

A voyeur I to what I saw,
But not from mere temptation.
For moaned and sighed they groaned and cried,
In their hyperventilation.

The sheets were crumbled and strewn about,
The duvet all a twitch.
I almost gave a mighty shout,
At the downright filthy bitch.

And then they reached the final thrust,
In a tremulous ghastly sensation.
That shook the bed with the power of lust,
In tumultuous exultation.

I threw a switch and ran inside,
And grabbed my walking stick.
To thrash their raw and naked hide,
'Till both of them were sick.

Their speed did match their act so cheap,
And I was bid farewell.
To later find them fast asleep,
Outside in their kennel.

John Fitzgerald
The Five Past Man

I

I am the five-past-man
Never there
On time I swear
No matter what I do
I'm due
To be no sooner
Than the five minutes late
It takes to be
The five-past-man I am.

II

Resolutions taken
To making
Time by having time
And not be late
Like five past eight
When all that's needed
Is five minutes ceded
To stretching limbs
And silly whims
As there I lay
In bed each day
Then face the rush
And final push
To face my fate
Five minutes late.

III

For I have tried
And often lied
To try explain
And dodge the blame
That though it seems

I do not care
There's many more like me
Will share
This awful state
Of being late
At any rate
While other's wait.

IV

The five-past-man
Who cannot change
Or re-arrange
His life to fit
The five minutes bit
That makes my life
So full of stress
I guess-
The man I am
Will always be
The five-past-man

V

For only dreams
Can make of me
What I would be
If time could rule
Like time in school
And turn my nature
Upside down
For nothing else
In my life can
Make me be
The five-to-man.

John Fitzgerald
The Stairs

Did the stairs creak beneath weighty step?
Aided by your fearful fret.
On silence depended your hopeful escape,
Tippy-toed darkness familiar of late.

Ascending the steps from bottom to top,
Was expertly done with hardly a stop.
Counting each step with mathematical care,
Oh the sixth and the seventh the giveaway pair.

Indiscreetly positioning a toe on these two,
Alerted the sleepers to one overdue.
So cleverly dodging this treacherous trap,
Was like a teetotaller with a nightcap.

Weaving and wobbling and holding the rail,
All were important for one not to fail.
Reaching the landing and a breather was had,
Now for the room that held Mam and Dad.

A door never closed but always ajar,
Your sanctuary's proximity so near yet so far.
Bracing yourself with only one thought,
To silently rest on the bed that you sought.

A rustling of blankets and a voice that was clear,
Froze you in space with terrorised fear.
With breath that was held and wild thumping heart,
Attaining your room at night was an art.

Was it a censure a call to explain,
Or words that were spoken in dreams of disdain.
You hoped for the latter but expected the worst,
For if it was true your efforts were cursed.

But sometimes it happened that sounds trailed away,
And reaching your room you mouthed 'hooray'.

Biographies

Anne-Marie Magorrian
Anne Marie Magorrian is a native of County Down, she now lives in Ballyneale, Carrick-on-Suir, Co. Tipperary. She is a homemaker and mother of two young children. Her interests are creative writing and journalism.

Mary O'Gorman
Grew up in Killarney but as her grandfather was from Sologheadbeg, she had strong Tipperary connections even then. Works as a counsellor in Loreto, Clonmel. An award-winning poet, her first collection *Barking at Blackbirds* was published in 2001.

Sam Greene
Born in Dublin 1963, shortlisted for the PJ O'Connor award at RTÉ in 2001. Wrote 55 episodes of "The Ryans" soap opera broadcast on Tipp Fm in 2002. First play, "A few close Friends" performed in Clonmel in 2003.

Emir Kelly
Originally from Wexford. Now calls the Comeraghs her home where she lives in Rathgormack with her sons on the family farm.

Noel Greaney
Originally from Mayo, Noel moved to Clonmel two years ago. He is very interested in traditional music and poetry.

Shauna McGarry Egan
Shauna McGarry Egan, is a secondary School Teacher. Shauna won third prize in a short story competition run by magazine Womans Way in 1995.

David Power
David Power, a Tipperary resident, is an English teacher and has taught at Rockwell College for over thirty years. He enjoys travel, reading and writing. In his youth he taught in Nigeria and Canada.

Derbhile Dromey

A native of Clonmel, Derbhile Dromey has been scribbling enthusiastically since her teens. She is qualified in journalism and has been working in radio for the past few years. Her ambition is to write and publish full length novels.

Paddy Phelan

Paddy Phelan is a founding member of the Cluain Meala Writers' Group. He has won numerous prizes for his limericks and verse.

Jenni Rope

Jenni Rope was born in Derbyshire, completed her BA (Hons) English Degree in London where she met her partner Brian. They settled in Ireland in 1999. Jenni is currently undertaking a postgraduate course in Arts Administration. This is her first time to be published.

Majella Whelan

Majella Whelan is from Clonmel and works as a secondary school teacher in Fethard. The extract here is taken from her first novel, *Prelude*, which she has just completed.

John Fitzgerald

My enjoyment of writing has left me no choice but to share some of my recent work with you. I hope you find these pieces provocative, hilarious, familiar and of course forgettable. Any similarity with works of previous winners of the Nobel Prize for Literature is purely coincidental and I'm sure, unintentional on their part.

63

Cluain Meala Writers

would like to thank the following, without whom
this Anthology would not have been possible.

List of Patrons

Tipperary (S.R.) County Council

Merck Sharp & Dohme

Kentz Group, Gortnafleur, Clonmel

The Crescent Stores, Clonmel

The Apple Farm, Moorstown, Cahir